For my parents, Marion and Lyndon Grove,
and in memory of my grandparents, Pearl and Bill Baker, and Helen and Jack Grove.

Acknowledgements

This book would not have been possible without the help of many people. I am grateful for the contribution of each.

I thankfully acknowledge the financial assistance of Canada Heritage and Canada Heritage Minister Sheila Copps.

For invaluable advice and expert review of my manuscript, I thank Trevor Mills, Archivist and train aficionado at West Coast Railway Heritage Park, Squamish, BC; Ted Palmer, Canadian historian and teacher, Madeira Park, BC; and Jean-Paul Viaud, Curator at the Canadian Railway Museum, Montreal. In particular, I would like to thank Robert Turner, author and railway enthusiast, for checking the text and art, and for providing visual references from his extensive personal collection. His assistance was much appreciated. Thank you to Arni Brownstone, Department of Anthropology, Royal Ontario Museum, for his checking of Métis and Aboriginal art. Thank you also to Judith Nevsky, Head Archivist, and to Bob Kennell, both of the Canadian Pacific Archives, Montreal, and Marnie Pickard of the Agassiz Harrison Museum for help in locating reference materials and sources.

In addition, I am grateful to my editor, Val Wyatt; my publisher, Valerie Hussey; and my colleague Linda Bailey, all of whom make my writing life possible.

An enormous thank you to my husband, Dave, and children, Emily, Mike and Helen, who graciously spent summer vacations visiting railway museums and kept me "on track" when the writing got tough.

Special recognition goes to my grandparents: To Bill Baker, who worked 49 years for the CPR, first as a wiper, then as a fireman and, finally, as an engineer with an impeccable safety record. To Jack Grove, who spent three decades with the CPR, first as Secretary to the General Superintendent and then as Senior Clerk in the General Superintendent's Office. And to Helen Bigler Grove, who was an Executive Secretary for the CPR.

Most importantly, thank you to my parents, Marion and Lyndon Grove, who grew up travelling across Canada on the CPR and whose knowledge and enthusiasm for train travel were the inspiration for this book.—D. H.

The illustrator is indebted to the many photographers of early trains for preserving this part of Canada's history. Extensive use has been made of these photographic references to ensure accuracy and the right period feel.—J. M.

Sources

The following images were reproduced by permission of Canadian Pacific Archives: **p. 12** poster, Image no. A. 6366; **p. 21** telegram, Image no. A. 93; **p. 23** poster, Image no. A. 6406; **p. 25**, train orders, Image no. BR. 209; **p. 31** timetable, top of page, Image no. BR. 210; **p. 31** poster, bottom of page, Image no. A. 6350; **p. 33** cover of menu, Image no. A. 99; **p. 33** inside menu, Image no. A. 100.

The following print sources have also been used:

p. 7 traveller's letter: *British Columbia and Vancouver's Island* by Duncan George Forbes MacDonald CE, p. 412. London: Longman, Green, Longman, Roberts and Green, 1862. **p. 8** Charlie Shaw quote: *Canadian Pacific Staff Bulletin,* Feb. 1, 1936. **p. 9** R.M. Rylatt quote: *Surveying the Canadian Pacific: Memoirs of a Railroad Pioneer* by R. M. Rylatt, p. 33, Salt Lake City: University of Utah Press, Tanner Trust Fund, 1991. **p. 12** End of Track quote: *When the Steel Went Through: Reminiscences of a Railroad Pioneer* by P. Turner Bone, p. 43. Toronto: MacMillan, 1947. **p. 14** Queenie Pink quote: letter to the author.

p. 19 Crowfoot quote: *Portraits from the Plains* by J.W. Grant MacEwen, p. 79. Toronto, New York: McGraw-Hill, 1971.

p. 22 spectator's quote: *Van Horne's Road* by Omer Lavallee, p. 275. Montreal: Railfare Enterprises, 1974.

p. 23 passenger's quote: *The Canadian Pacific Railway: The New Highway to the East Across the Mountains, Prairies and Rivers of Canada,* p. 15, Montreal: Railfare Enterprises, 1887. **p. 30** Helen Bigler's quote: letter belonging to the author's family.

Kids Can Press acknowledges the financial support of the Ontario Arts Council, the Canada Council for the Arts and the Government of Canada, through the BPIDP, for our publishing activity.

This project has been supported by the Canadian Studies and Special Projects Directorate, Canada Heritage. The opinions expressed do not necessarily reflect the view of the Government of Canada.

Published in Canada by
Kids Can Press Ltd.
29 Birch Avenue
Toronto, ON M4V 1E2

Published in the U.S. by
Kids Can Press Ltd.
4500 Witmer Estates
Niagara Falls, NY 14305-1386

Edited by Valerie Wyatt
Designed by Julia Naimska
Printed in Hong Kong
by Wing King Tong Company Limited

CM 00 0 9 8 7 6 5 4 3 2 1

Canadian Cataloguing in Publication Data

Hodge, Deborah
The kids book of Canada's railway : and how the CPR was built

Includes index.
ISBN 1-55074-526-3

1. Canadian Pacific Railway Company — History — Juvenile literature. 2. Railroads — Canada — History — Juvenile literature. 3. Canada — History — 1867–   . — Juvenile literature. I. Mantha, John. II. Title.

HE2810.C2H557 2000   j385'.0971   C99-932726-7

Kids Can Press is a Nelvana company

CONTENTS

STEP BACK IN TIME

Meet Catherine Schubert and her family. They journeyed across Canada in 1862 with a group of people called the Overlanders — some of the first settlers to cross the country by land. Catherine was the only woman in the group of about 150 travellers.

Setting off in a procession of Red River carts and ending up on foot, they trekked 5600 km (3500 mi.) from Fort Garry (now Winnipeg) to the Cariboo goldfields of British Columbia. The journey took almost five months. There were no roads or bridges, just wilderness. Along the way, they built bridges or swam across rivers, cut trails through forests and hiked over mountain passes. They endured fierce weather and near starvation. On the final leg of their journey, the Overlanders rafted down the Thompson River. Some people drowned in the churning water, but the Schuberts made it safely to Fort Kamloops. Hours later, Catherine gave birth to a healthy baby girl.

Catherine Schubert and the Overlanders

If you could travel back to Catherine Schubert's time, you would find a very different Canada than the country we know today. Instead of cities linked by roads and railways, the land was wild and untamed. Instead of provinces and territories joined under one government, there were settlements in the east and west. A huge stretch of prairie, lakes and rocky Canadian Shield lay between them. The total population was only about one-tenth of what it is today.

Twenty-five years after Catherine Schubert's journey, everything began to change. Towns and cities sprang up across the land. Industries grew and the population swelled. Why the change? A railway had been built across the country, linking east and west and opening up the country for European settlers.

This is the story of that railway and of the people who built it.

Canada in 1860

For thousands of years, Canada's only inhabitants were the Aboriginal people. Then, in the 1800s, large numbers of newcomers began to arrive. In the east came people from Britain and France who settled on farms or in cities such as Montreal and Halifax. In the west, prospectors arrived in British Columbia for the Cariboo goldrush of 1860–1866 and stayed on. The way of life for Aboriginal people began to change as these newcomers explored the country and settled in it.

Canoeing the Wilderness

Between east and west lay a deep wilderness — the forests, swamps, lakes and rock of the Canadian Shield. There was no way through this wilderness except by canoe. Travellers who wanted to get to the prairies took a train through the United States, then a riverboat north to Canada.

A RIBBON OF STEEL

Sir John A. Macdonald, Canada's first prime minister

In the 1860s, politicians in eastern Canada feared that large pieces of unsettled land in the north and west were going to be claimed by the United States. Much of the free land in the United States was gone, and American settlers were looking for new areas to stake. So the politicians in Canada came up with a plan to unite the colonies under one government. On July 1, 1867, the colonies of New Brunswick, Nova Scotia, Ontario and Quebec joined together to form the Dominion of Canada. This union was called Confederation, and Sir John A. Macdonald became the first prime minister.

Macdonald began the work of building up the country. He wanted to expand the Dominion of Canada from sea to sea and fill the land with settlers and farms. In a time when the lines of communication and travel ran from north to south, he needed a way to link east with west. A cross-country railway was the solution. Macdonald promised to build one if British Columbia would join Confederation. The province joined in 1871.

Many believed it would be impossible to build a railway across 3200 km (2000 mi.) of mountains, prairies, rivers and swamps, but Macdonald was determined to see it through. When he realized how expensive the project would be, he found a partner, a private group called the Canadian Pacific Railway (CPR). By 1881, the CPR was ready to start building Canada's first transcontinental railway — a ribbon of steel to span the country.

The Dorchester

There were railways in Canada before the transcontinental. The first official railway, built in 1836, ran between the St. Lawrence and Richelieu Rivers. It was less than 25 km (15 mi.) long. The Dorchester was the first locomotive to run on the new track. The initial trips were made at night to avoid scaring people. Most had never seen a steam engine before. These early locomotives were called "iron horses."

The Railway Comes to Town

By 1860, more railways had been built in Ontario, Quebec and the Maritimes. People were so excited about the first train coming to town that stores were closed and holidays declared. Dressed in their best clothes, townspeople would crowd the station platform to greet the train. Speeches were made and parades were held. The entire town celebrated.

A Traveller's Letter

In 1862, before the transcontinental railway was built, an English traveller made a seven-month journey from Red River (now Manitoba) to Victoria, British Columbia. Here is part of his letter home.

Day after day, travelling in mud and water, in some places so deep that carts and horses were well-nigh disappearing altogether ... we had to wade through the mud and water and put our shoulders to the wheels; and I think you would have scarcely known me under the thick coating of black mud ... The mosquitoes tormented us almost to madness; no rest did they give us day or night ...

Our provisions ran out ... For several days we existed upon roseberries; they are rather woolly eating but we had excellent appetites — so much so, that we killed my poor dog ... we ate him ravenously ... After the dog was finished, we fasted a few days ... but we became so weak we were obliged to kill a horse. As soon as he dropped, each cut a piece and threw it into the fire; my partner did not wait to cook his, but ate it raw. We ate more that day than we had eaten for three weeks previous ...

SURVEYING THE LAND

Surveyor Charlie Shaw

Meet Charlie Shaw. At age 18, he joined one of 21 survey crews criss-crossing the country. It was their job to find the safest, least expensive and most direct route for the railway.

Charlie describes his first winter on a survey team. The crew was boating across Lake Superior in 1871 to begin surveying west of Port Arthur (now Thunder Bay): "Each night we ... camped. We had been cheated on our blankets and they weren't much good. It was as cold as 52 below at times. Each night half a party stayed up to keep the fires going. We reached Port Arthur on January 9, a month less a day from the start. We worked westward all winter, hauling our supplies in by dog team. Our ration was flour, beans and Chicago 'mess pork,' noted for its inches of fat and minimum of lean."

Each survey crew had an engineer. He walked ahead of the crew to mark possible routes. He looked for the easiest route and tried to avoid spots that would need tunnels or bridges.

Workers with axes chopped out a path for the surveyors coming behind. The surveyors used long survey chains and special instruments to measure the land. They drew maps of each area.

The survey crews had to be strong and tough. In summer, the heat was fierce and the insects were bloodthirsty. In winter, the cold and wind cut through their tents. And always, the land was rugged. Climbing mountains, fording rivers and wading through swamps was part of the job.

Some surveyors died in forest fires. Others drowned. Many were injured or got sunstroke, frostbite or scurvy. Some men tangled with grizzly bears, rattlesnakes and other wild animals. On top of that, surveying was lonely work. Surveyors often spent years away from their families, with little news of home.

The Final Route of the CPR

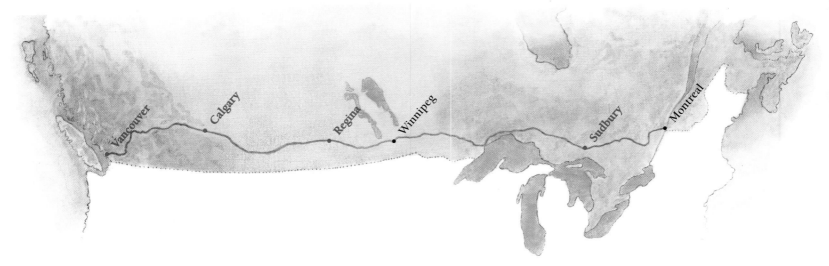

Much of the railway survey was completed by 1877. By then, surveyors had covered more than 19 000 km (12 000 mi.) of Canadian wilderness on foot. But the final route for the transcontinental railway, shown above, was not chosen until 1881.

Cities shown in red were founded after the railway was built.

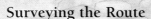

Sandford Fleming, Engineer

In 1871, Sandford Fleming was hired as chief engineer of the Pacific Railway Survey. He divided the country into three sections and sent out survey crews to each. It took the surveyors about six years to measure and mark the land from Ontario to British Columbia.

Surveying the Route

Surveyors had to find the flattest ground along the shortest route. Crews used long survey chains to divide the route into 30 m (100 ft.) lengths. They hammered in stakes to mark each length. An instrument called a transit (shown above) was used to measure the angles between landmarks. It helped surveyors calculate distances.

Raft Overturned!

R.M. Rylatt and his survey crew were rafting down the Columbia River when they suddenly came upon a set of rapids: "We were forced too near shore on our unwieldy craft ... before we could avoid the danger [we] came full tilt against a fallen tree, half submerged and projecting out into the current. All leaped for dear life when close upon it, and clung desperately to the slimy log. Jas Maloney leapt short however, and he and the raft were both sucked under. We never saw him again."

LAYING TRACK

The CPR's general manager, Van Horne, was famous for saying such things as, "Nothing is too small to know, and nothing is too big to attempt."

By 1881, the survey was finished and the route was chosen. It was time to start laying the track. In order to finish the railway as quickly as possible, construction was started from both ends — from the east and from the west.

An American named William Cornelius Van Horne was hired to oversee the job. He worked hard, slept little and expected everyone else to do the same. Van Horne pledged to build 800 km (500 mi.) of track the first summer, breaking a speed record for railway building. To accomplish this feat, he needed the help of navvies — workers who got their name from the early builders of navigation canals.

Before the track could be laid, crews of navvies cut trees and cleared a wide path on both sides of the staked line left by the surveyors. The crews used teams of animals pulling scrapers and plows to level the roadbed over which the trains would travel.

While the roadbed was being cleared, bridge-building crews constructed bridges and trestles across rivers and canyons. Blasting crews used black powder and dynamite to tunnel through rock.

Once the roadbed was ready, track-laying crews followed. Wooden railway ties were laid across the roadbed. The distance between the ties — 61 cm (2 ft.) — was carefully measured.

Steel rails 12 m (39 ft.) long were laid on either side of the ties. Iron spikes were hammered in to hold the rails in place. Ballast (gravel and soil) was spread onto the roadbed to make the track steady and stable. Everything was done by hand.

William Van Horne came just short of reaching his goal of building 800 km (500 mi.) of track the first summer. Flooding of the Red River had thwarted him. But he and his navvies had succeeded in laying 772 km (480 mi.) of track across the prairies in only a few months. The job involved 5000 men and 1700 teams of horses. Piece by piece and spike by spike, the ribbon of steel began to snake across the countryside.

The surveyors marked the route.

The navvies cleared a wide swath on both sides of the route.

Grading crews levelled the roadbed.

Raising a Telegraph Pole

Following the track-layers came the crews who strung up telegraph wires on poles along the tracks. Over these wires, messages called telegrams could be sent. The telegraph system meant that people at one end of the country could quickly communicate with those at the other end. This changed the way of life for early Canadians.

Joining the Rails

Rails were bolted together with flat metal plates called fishplates.

The Ties

Ties were cut from tree trunks.
Each tie was 2.5 m (8 ft.) long and very heavy.

Track-layers laid wooden ties on the roadbed.

Steel rails were laid on top and held in place with iron spikes.

Spaces between the ties were filled with gravel.

THE NAVVIES

On the prairies, navvies worked under the blazing sun, laying up to 8 km (5 mi.) of track a day. This was very fast in a time when everything was done by hand.

When the day was over, the weary men retired to train cars, called boarding cars, which served as their sleeping quarters. A cooking car and supply cars followed the workers down the line. This area was called End of Track, and it moved as each new section of track was laid.

As P. Turner Bone remembers: "End of Track was ... a real live community, a hive of industry, in which teamsters, track-layers, blacksmiths, carpenters, executive officers, and other trades and professions all had a part. They had their quarters on a train composed of cars loaded with rails and other track materials, followed by large boarding cars for the workmen, and by sundry smaller cars for the executives. This train was pushed ahead as the track laying proceeded; and at the end of a day's work, it might be three or four miles from where it was on the morning."

Many of the navvies who worked in Ontario and the prairies were newcomers to Canada from Italy, Ukraine, Poland, Sweden, Finland, Russia and Germany. On the west coast,

Workers on the railway were called navvies.

many workers came from China (for more about them, turn the page). While English-speaking Canadians often built bridges and worked with machinery, much of the track-laying was done by men from other countries.

A navvy's earnings ranged from $1.00 to $1.50 a day in the east and from $2.00 to $2.50 a day on the prairies. (A dollar a day was a standard rate for physical labour in those days.) From this wage, a navvy had to pay for food, clothing, blankets, rail transportation to the job site, mail and medical expenses. If the weather was poor and work was halted, the navvies were not paid — yet they still had to pay for food and expenses. After two and a half months of work, a navvy might end up with as little as $16.00 in his pocket. Working

on the railway was not an easy way to get rich. Even so, the job was appealing because it was steady work — something rare in those times.

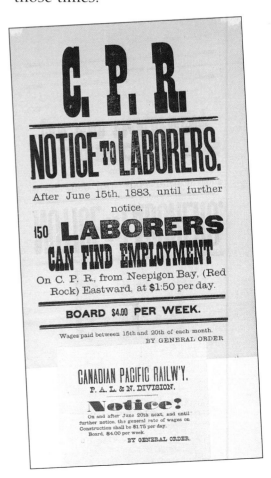

C. P. R.

NOTICE TO LABORERS.

After June 15th, 1883, until further notice,

150 LABORERS CAN FIND EMPLOYMENT

On C. P. R., from Neepigon Bay, (Red Rock) Eastward, at $1.50 per day.

BOARD $4.00 PER WEEK.

Wages paid between 15th and 20th of each month.

BY GENERAL ORDER.

CANADIAN PACIFIC RAILW'Y.
P. A. L. & N. DIVISION.

Notice!

On and after June 20th next, and until further notice, the general rate of wages on Construction shall be $1.75 per day.
Board, $4.00 per week.

BY GENERAL ORDER.

End of Track
The prairie navvies slept in two- or three-storey-high train cars. Sometimes tents were pitched on the roofs.

Inside a Bunkhouse
Many navvies in Ontario lived in construction camps. At these camps, the men often slept in dingy, windowless bunkhouses with 60 to 80 other workers. They were known as "bunkhouse men."

Cooking for the Camp
Bread was baked in a stone oven at some construction camps. Fresh bread was a treat for hungry workers. Most often they ate a simple diet of beans, salt pork, potatoes and oatmeal — food that kept well during long periods in the bush.

13

WEST COAST NAVVIES

Railway navvy Pon Git Cheng

Meet Pon Git Cheng. He was one of thousands of workers who travelled from China by boat in 1882. They came to help build the western sections of the railway in British Columbia. These sections, through mountains and over rivers, were extremely difficult to build. There weren't enough local workers to do the job, so workers from other countries were hired.

Like many others, Pon Git Cheng was hoping to earn enough money in Canada to support his family back home. Unfortunately, the Chinese navvies were paid little — only about $.75 to $1.25 a day. After paying for transportation, food and clothing, there was little money to send home. In fact, when the railway was completed, many navvies could not even afford to return to China.

The Chinese navvies were not used to the cold climate or the food. They suffered from exposure and scurvy. They were looked down on by many of the other workers and were often given the hardest or most dangerous jobs. They cleared away rock from the blasting sites and shovelled ballast onto the tracks. They worked with dangerous explosives, climbed cliffs, and were injured in rock slides and falls. At least 600 Chinese workers died in accidents or of illness while building the railway.

Fong Chong, a labour agent from Agassiz, British Columbia, helped bring the men from China to work on the railway. His granddaughter, Queenie Pink, remembers: "There was no compensation for the men's families in China for the lost lives and no notification of loss of life. The men who lived did not have enough money to return to their wives and families in China, and many spent their years in lonely, sad and often poor conditions."

The Chinese navvies were reliable, hard-working men whom the railway contractors came to depend on. Their back-breaking efforts played a key role in building the western stretch of the railway.

Chinese Navvies

About two-thirds of the navvies in British Columbia were Chinese. They lived in their own camps. English-speaking workers did not mix with them.

Boys as young as 12 came to work on the railway. They served as tea-boys on the Chinese crews.

Pulling the *Skuzzy*

It was September 28, 1882, and Supervisor Andrew Onderdonk was having trouble moving a supply boat, the *Skuzzy*, up Hell's Gate — a deep, narrow channel of the Fraser River known for its rapids and rocks. After days of trying and failing, Onderdonk had ring bolts drilled into the sides of the rocky canyon and thick ropes slipped through them. These ropes were attached to the boat. He lined up 150 Chinese workers on the sides of the rocky bank and ordered them to pull. Little by little, the heavy boat moved upstream. When news of the success reached the nearby town of Yale, a celebration was declared.

Andrew Onderdonk

Onderdonk supervised much of the railway construction in British Columbia from 1880–85. His workers built 27 tunnels through mountains and 600 bridges and trestles over steep canyons and churning rivers.

DANGEROUS WORK

Navvies in the east blasted through some of the hardest, oldest rock in the world, the Canadian Shield. The work north of Lake Superior was so difficult that Van Horne called it "200 miles of engineering impossibility." As well as rock, there were huge stretches of muskeg — deep boggy patches that sometimes swallowed entire stretches of track.

Some crews worked right through the winter. Even snowstorms and bone-chilling temperatures of -40°C (-40°F) didn't stop them. Summers weren't much better, with temperatures rising to 30°C (90°F) and swarms of mosquitoes and flies that never stopped biting.

In the west, crews tunnelled through mountains that stood in their way. Men were lowered on ropes down sheer cliffs to drill holes and set explosive charges. Dynamite or a mixture of black powder and nitroglycerine were tamped into the holes and ignited. If something went wrong, there were rock slides and falls — and sometimes deaths.

Crossing rivers was another challenge. Before the track could be laid, massive wooden trestles and bridges had to be built over canyons and rivers. Bridge-builders often worked at dizzying heights with rivers swirling below. To slip and fall meant certain death. In spite of the danger, hundreds of bridges and trestles were built through the mountains. These impressive structures were admired by engineers around the world.

Cutting Through the Mountains
Mountain crews were suspended by ropes. Perched in rows, they dug tunnels into the rock. Men on the top row would holler, "Look out below!" as streams of rocks and boulders hurtled towards the men beneath them.

Crossing Canyons

In the Selkirk Mountains, deep canyons cut through steep mountains. A series of bridges and trestles, such as the one shown here, were built from timber cut in nearby forests.

THE INLAND SENTINEL

Yale, B.C., Thursday, June 9, 1881. No.2

THE BIG TUNNEL ACCIDENT

A very sad accident occurred at the Big Tunnel this morning a few minutes past 6 o'clock a.m., wherein two men were instantly killed by a large rock falling from the roof of a tunnel upon them. David McKay, one of the victims, had his head almost bruised to a jelly and turned to one side, but strange to say that the flesh was not cut … John Carson, (or better known as Rocky Mountain Jack,) had his head cut, body badly bruised and both legs crushed … This accident cast a sad melancholy gloom over the place for the time being.

In Memory

Railway-building was a risky business. This burial site was a memorial to a navvy who died on the job. The sign says "Died on the Railroad."

BATTLE ON THE PRAIRIES

By 1885, with just a few hundred kilometres (miles) of track remaining to be built, the railway ground to a halt. The CPR had run out of money. Then William Van Horne heard about a conflict brewing on the prairies, and he came up with an idea of how the railway might help the government — and get the money needed to finish the track.

The conflict, known as the Northwest Rebellion, had broken out because the Métis (people of Aboriginal and European background) felt their rights to the land were being taken away by the government. So did the Blackfoot, Cree and other Aboriginal people who had been pressured to move onto reserves (small tracts of land to be farmed). The government wanted the prairie lands for the railway and to attract new settlers. The Métis and Aboriginal people understood that the coming of the railway threatened their way of life. They knew it had happened

Louis Riel (left) was a gifted speaker who fought tirelessly for the rights of the Métis. Gabriel Dumont (right) was a shrewd military commander.

in the United States.

Led by Louis Riel and Gabriel Dumont, Métis and some Aboriginal warriors clashed with the North West Mounted Police. The government in Ottawa decided to send troops. That's when Van Horne stepped in. He offered to use the new railway

to move 3000 troops by train.

Even though the railway was unfinished, the soldiers were at the battle lines in a week. Fierce fighting lasted for several days. In the end, the warriors were defeated by the government troops. Louis Riel was captured and later put to death. Gabriel Dumont escaped to the United States. Cree chiefs Big Bear and Poundmaker, who had advised their people not to join the battle, were nonetheless put in jail. The Rebellion was over.

The railway had proved its worth to the government. It loaned the CPR money to finish building the track. Six months later, it was completed.

While the show of speed and strength was good for the government and the CPR, it was a great tragedy for the Métis and Aboriginal people. The coming of the railway changed their lives forever. The land and the buffalo they depended on were gone. The government, the railway and the settlers were there to stay.

Cree Leaders

Even though they had advised their people not to fight, Cree leaders Big Bear (left) and Poundmaker (right) were thrown in jail. The government held them responsible for their peoples' participation in the rebellion.

Chief Crowfoot

When government officials tried to bargain for rights to the prairie lands, this Blackfoot leader said, "Our land is more valuable than your money. It will last forever. It will not perish as long as the sun shines and the water flows … It was put there by the Great Spirit and we cannot sell it because it does not belong to us."

Battle at Batoche

It was at Batoche on May 9–12, 1885, that the Métis and Aboriginal warriors were finally defeated by government troops.

Transporting the Troops

Although parts of the railway north of Lake Superior were unfinished, the troops still travelled to Qu'Appelle, in what is now Saskatchewan, in the record time of seven days. Before the railway, a similar trip had taken three months.

Buffalo Bones

For thousands of years, Aboriginal people depended on herds of buffalo that roamed the prairies. But by 1880, the buffalo had almost disappeared — they had been overhunted, and settlers were moving into buffalo territory. All that was left were piles of bones. Without the buffalo to hunt, the Aboriginal people were starving. They had no choice but to move onto reserve lands offered by the government. This move was extremely difficult for them. They had no farming experience and felt that farming was unworthy of warrior-hunters.

THE LAST SPIKE

At 9:22 A.M. on November 7, 1885, a plain iron spike was hammered into place at Craigellachie, British Columbia. The spike was like the many thousands used to build the railway. But it was also a very special spike — it was the last spike, joining the two parts of the transcontinental railway.

The spike was hammered into place by railway official Donald Smith. For a few seconds afterwards, the air was heavy with silence. Then wild cheering and clapping broke out, and the crowd shouted for William Van Horne to make a speech. The general manager of the CPR, who had been a fierce and unrelenting boss over the past five years, did not waste words. He spoke only one sentence: "All I can say is that the work has been done well in every way."

It was a historic day in Canada. The longest, most expensive, most challenging railway in the world had been built faster than anyone thought possible. Thanks to the determination of William Van Horne and the strong backs of the navvies, the dream of a transcontinental railway had become a reality. The entire nation from the Atlantic to the Pacific Ocean was now joined up by an iron road that would allow people to travel, trade and communicate as never before.

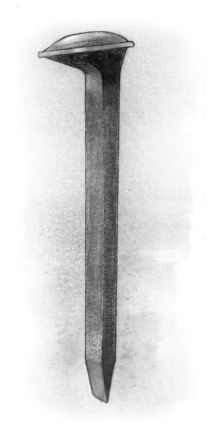

It took millions of these spikes to lay the tracks across Canada.

The Task Is Finished

When the navvies laid down their tools for the last time, construction of nearly 3200 km (2000 mi.) of track through muskeg and Canadian Shield, across the prairies and over the mountains had been accomplished in four and a half years. It had taken 30 000 workers to do the job.

TELEGRAM.

Rt Hon Sir
J. A. MacDonald
KCB

From Craigellachie Eagle pass BC

Thanks to your far seeing policy and unwavering support the Canadian Pacific Railway is completed the last rail was laid this (Saturday) morning at 9.22

W. C. VanHorne

The First Transcontinental

After the ceremony, William Van Horne, Donald Smith and other railway officials boarded a special train that had come from Montreal and was bound for Port Moody, British Columbia. This train was the first one ever to travel from Montreal to the Pacific Ocean. It arrived in Port Moody on November 8, 1885. But the first passenger train was yet to come ...

THE FIRST TRAIN

At 12:00 noon on July 4, 1886, the Pacific Express rolled into the station at Port Moody, British Columbia. Carrying 150 people, it was the first passenger train to make the cross-Canada trip.

Excited crowds, including the mayors of Victoria and Vancouver, gathered at the railway station to greet the Pacific Express.

According to one spectator, "First a whistle was heard, and then the old familiar curl of smoke was to be seen rising from among the pines; then came the harsh clang clang of the engined bell and the train slowly steamed up the line and was greeted by cheer after cheer from the 500 or 600 people who were awaiting her."

The Pacific Express had crossed the entire breadth of the country, from Quebec to British Columbia. Travelling at an average speed of 35 km/h (21 m.p.h), it had covered nearly 4700 km (2900 mi.) in just 5 days and 19 hours.

On that historic rail trip, the train began its journey with baggage and mail cars, two colonist cars, the "Holyrood" dining car, two first-class coaches and two sleepers named the "Honolulu" and "Yokohama."

Twenty-six engines took turns hauling the cars. During the trip, the train burned 520 cords of fire wood — enough wood to fill a hockey rink up to the boards.

At every station stop along the way, curious crowds boarded the train to look at the lavish first-class cars. They were impressed by the mahogany wood, stained glass windows, lush carpets, thick curtains and up-to-date plumbing with hot and cold running water. These cars were much fancier than what most people were used to. Many did not yet have indoor plumbing or running water in their homes.

A Red Letter Day For • Canada June 28, '86 WHEN THE CANADIAN PACIFIC RAILWAY OPENS PACIFIC OCEAN —TO THE—

TRAIN LEAVES DAILY:

Toronto, - - 5.00 p.m. (17 O'CLOCK)
Montreal, - - 8.00 " (20 O'CLOCK)
Ottawa, - - 11.45 " (23.45 O'CLOCK)
EXCEPT SUNDAY

OUR OWN LINE —FROM THE— ATLANTIC TO THE PACIFIC

NO CUSTOMS   NO DELAYS   NO TRANSFERS
LOW RATES   QUICK TIME

For further particulars apply to any Agent of the Company, or to
W. D. HUGHES,
Travelling Passenger Agent.
W. R. CALLAWAY,
District Passenger Agent.
110 KING STREET WEST, TORONTO

W. C. VAN HORNE
Vice-President
GEO. OLDS
Gen. Traffic Manager
MONTREAL
D. McNICOLL
General Pass. Agent

McKay Bros., Printers, Toronto

Riding the Cowcatcher

On July 9, 1886, Agnes Macdonald and her husband, Prime Minister Sir John A. Macdonald, rode a special train from Ottawa to British Columbia. To get the best view, Agnes rode for a short distance on the cowcatcher. It was a metal frame at the front of the train that pushes obstructions — including cows — off the track. After that, the cowcatcher became a fashionable (but dangerous) viewing spot for special passengers, including visiting royalty.

Luxury on Rails

In the words of one early passenger, "Our sleeping car ... [has] soft and rich cushions, silken curtains, thick carpets, delicate carvings and beautiful decorations ... it gives us promise of a delightful journey."

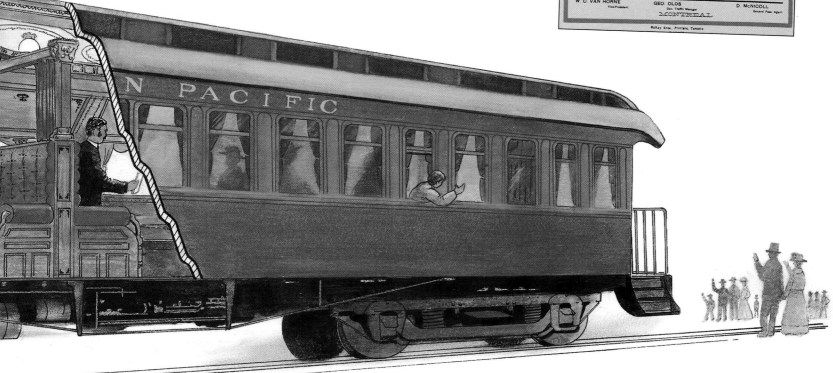

THE RAILWAY STATION

Railway stations were built about every 13 km (8 mi.) along the railway line. The trains stopped at these stations to pick up passengers, freight and mail.

In many places where the stations were built, new towns sprang up. Everyone wanted to be close to the railway line. The land was valuable because being close to the railway was good for business. In fact, when the railway bypassed them, some towns even moved to be closer to it.

At the Station

The railway station was a busy place. In the early years, it was often the centre of the community. Passengers arrived and departed. Mail and cargo were loaded and unloaded. Telegraph messages were sent.

When the train was ready to leave the station, the conductor called out, "All aboard."

At large stations, the passengers' luggage was loaded into the baggage car by a baggage handler.

Train Orders

Train orders were telegraphed to the station by a dispatcher, who scheduled the runs of all the trains in an area. These special instructions were so important that a train could not leave the station without them. Train orders told the engineer and conductor when to depart, what speed to travel, where to stop and gave information about accidents or delays. They were critical in preventing trains from colliding.

The station agent's family often lived upstairs.

In the early days, every town used a slightly different time. Sandford Fleming realized this would be confusing once the trains were running, so he came up with a system of standard time, which divided the world into 24 equal time zones. We still use this system today. To honour this innovation, Sandford Fleming was knighted.

The station agent operated the telegraph, sending and receiving telegrams written in Morse code and transmitted over telegraph wires. Both the public and the railway company relied on the telegraph system.

The station agent sold tickets and kept track of the train schedule.

THE ENGINE

Early trains were powered by steam. Water in the steam engine's boiler was heated by a fire fuelled with coal or wood. As the water boiled, it turned into steam. The steam was piped to the cylinders, where it expanded, causing parts called pistons to move back and forth. The pistons were connected to long arms called driving rods, which turned the wheels. The train cars were pulled along the track by this great hissing steam engine.

A large steam engine burned up to 15 tonnes (tons) of coal to travel 200 km (125 mi.) through the mountains. So fuel had to be replaced often. Coal or wood and water were picked up at divisional points — special servicing spots located every 200 km (125 mi.) along the line. Water for the boiler was needed more often — in some places every 16 km (10 mi.).

An engine crew stayed with one engine, hauling trains along a certain section of track, called a subdivision. The divisional point was the turnaround place. When a train reached the divisional point, the crew uncoupled (unhooked) their engine and serviced it. (Another engine pulled the train to the next divisional point.) Once the engine was serviced, the crew coupled it to a train heading in the opposite direction and pulled it back across the subdivision.

A smokestack carried smoke up above the train, so that it wouldn't bother the passengers and engine crew.

A warning bell signalled people to move out of the way of the train.

Steam collected in the steam dome and was piped to the cylinders

Excess steam escaped from safety valves.

A headlight lit the way for the engineer at night and warned people that the train was coming.

The cowcatcher pushed obstructions — including cows — off the track.

Water was heated in the boiler.

The pistons pushed the driving rods.

Inside the Cab

The engineer used valves and controls to increase or decrease the amount of steam pressure moving through the engine. More steam meant more speed. He also applied the brakes when needed. Special gauges told him the amount of air in the brakes and water in the boiler. Other gauges showed how much steam had built up in the engine. If the water temperature was too cool, steam couldn't be produced. The fireman had to shovel more coal (or, in later trains, increase the flow of oil) into the fire box. Water also had to be added from time to time or the engine would explode. Driving a steam engine took skill, teamwork and fast thinking.

The sand dome held sand that was sprinkled on the track to provide traction for the train's wheels.

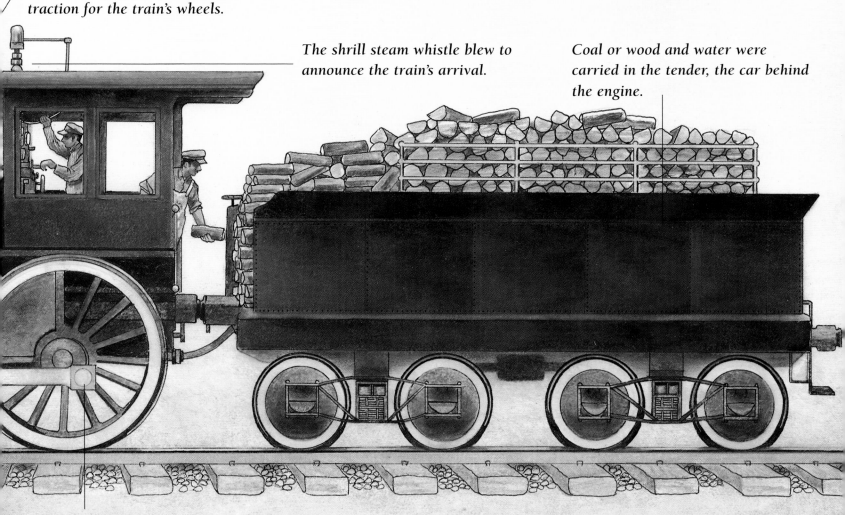

The shrill steam whistle blew to announce the train's arrival.

Coal or wood and water were carried in the tender, the car behind the engine.

The driving rods turned the wheels.

PASSENGER TRAINS

Meet Helen Bigler, who moved from Michigan to Saskatchewan with her family in 1907. "We came on the 'Homesteader's Train.' The journey was long and tiresome. There was no diner or sleeper on these trains. Everyone brought their own food, blankets, pillows and a good supply of medicine for any disease they might get in the new country."

The train was a new adventure for many Canadians. Never before had people been able to travel a long distance so quickly.

Depending on how much money passengers wished to pay, they could travel colonist class in plain colonist cars, second class in modest surroundings or first class in luxury cars.

Cars could be coupled (joined) and uncoupled (separated) at various points along the journey, so each train was different. But a typical order of cars on an early passenger train was the engine, mail car, baggage car, colonist car, coach, second class sleeper, dining car, first class sleeper and observation car. Passengers who could afford higher prices rode near the end of the train. Those with less money rode in colonist cars near the front of the train, close to the engine and baggage car.

In the early days, transcontinental passenger trains departed from the east and west two or three times a week. It took about six days for the train to cross the country.

The Colonist Car

Many settlers road to the prairies in colonist cars. It was an inexpensive way to travel a long distance. There were no luxuries in these cars. Passengers sat on hard, wooden seats, and slept in plain sleeping platforms, called "berths." The berths had no bedding, so people brought their own blankets. Hungry travellers cooked their own meals on pot-bellied stoves at either end of the car. These stoves provided the only heat in winter.

Settling the Prairies

The government wanted to fill the prairies with settlers, so they promised very cheap land to people who agreed to homestead (clear land and build a home). Thousands of newcomers poured into the area from Eastern Europe and other places.

In an almost treeless area, building a home was tough. Many settlers built sod houses like the one shown here. The settlers battled blizzards, hail storms, prairie fires, drought and loneliness.

The Coach

On short trips, passengers often rode in the coach. They could buy candy, fruit, sandwiches, coffee and cold drinks from the candy butcher (or news agent). He also sold newspapers and rented pillows to passengers.

The boss or captain of the train was the conductor. He took tickets and supervised the passengers and the train staff. The trainman was the conductor's assistant.

The Sleeping Car

Passengers making a long journey often rode in a sleeping car where the seats could be turned down into beds at night. Beds could also be pulled down from overhead. The porter made up the beds and helped make the passengers comfortable. Curtains were pulled across for the passengers' privacy.

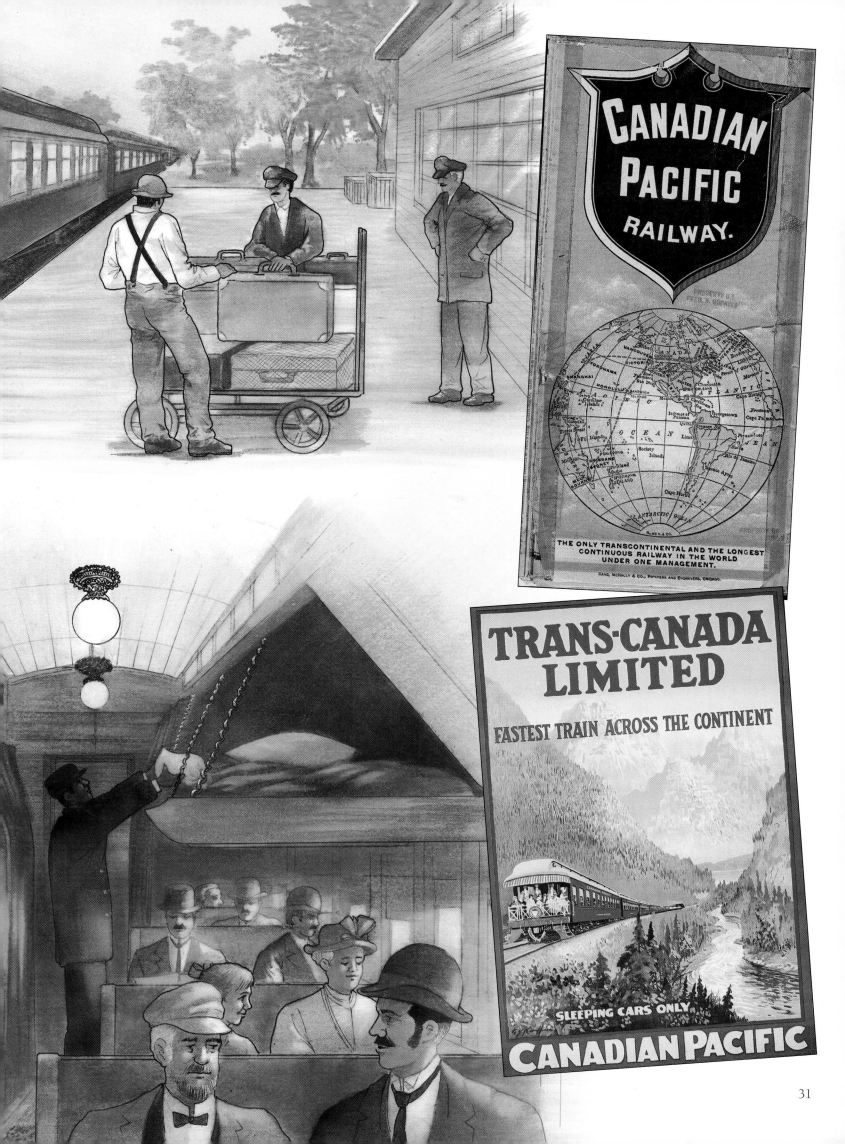

The Dining Car

Only those passengers who could afford the high prices ate in the dining car. The tables were set with fine china and crystal, white linen, freshly cut flowers and expensive silverware. Waiters served gourmet food prepared by some of the finest chefs in the country. The dining car steward supervised the cooks and waiters and made sure the customers were happy.

The Observation Car

Well-to-do travellers often rode through the mountains in an observation car. Here they had the best view of the breathtaking scenery. As William Van Horne said, "Since we can't export the scenery, we shall have to import the tourists."

➤ DINNER ✦

19th May 1886

Soup *Barley*

Fish.
Boiled Haddock & Cream Sauce
Boiled Leg of Mutton, Caper Sauce.
Boiled Ham.
Roast Turkey & Cranberry
Roast Beef.   Roast Lamb, Mint Sauce.

Entrees.
Fillet of Beef au Madeira
Stewed Lamb & Green Peas
Boiled and Mashed Potatoes.   ~~String Beans~~
~~Stewed Tomatoes~~   Mashed Turnips.
Green Corn & ~~Green Peas~~

Salad.

Water Biscuits.   Stilton Cheese.

Pastry.
Custard Pudding Apple
Blancmange
Green Tea.   Black English Breakfast Tea.
Chocolate.   Coffee.
Fruits.

MEALS 75 CENTS.

NEPIGON RIVER ON THE CANADIAN PACIFIC RAILWAY.

Canadian Pacific

RAILWAY DINING CAR
MENU

GEO. BISHOP ENG. & PT'G CO. MONTREAL.

Mountain Hotels

Fully loaded dining cars were heavy to move through the mountains. So hotels were built in mountain passes, and passengers would get off the trains to eat there. Later, grand resorts, such as the Banff Springs shown here, were built for wealthy tourists travelling by train.

MAINTAINING THE TRACK

The train cars and track needed constant maintenance and repair to keep the railway running smoothly.

The engines and train cars were serviced at divisional points. Here, the engine crews cleaned, polished and refuelled their locomotives. Major repairs to engines were done by mechanics in a roundhouse — a repair shop where locomotives were arranged in a circle or semicircle around a large turntable.

Sectionmen kept the track in good repair. A crew of four men was responsible for maintaining a section — about 13 km (8 mi.) long. The crew patrolled their

The trackwalker lived a lonely life in a shack by the side of the tracks. His only visitors were passing trains whose crews might toss him a stack of magazines or newspapers.

section of track every day, replacing damaged ties and rails. They kept the track level by shovelling gravel under the ties.

Tunnels were taken care of by a trackwalker who lived near the entrance to each major tunnel. The trackwalker's job was to maintain the track inside the tunnel and clear away obstacles such as fallen rock or ice. If conditions were dangerous, he signalled the trains to stop.

In the mountains, crews worked hard to keep the track clear of ice and snow. This was a neverending job in winter. Avalanches often buried the track and sometimes the track crew.

Gandy Dancers

Sectionmen were also called gandy dancers. The name came from tools made by the Gandy Manufacturing Company. Swinging these tools, crews moved in a steady rhythm — like dancers!

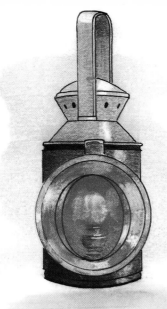

Warning!

If there was an obstruction on the track, a sectionman or trackwalker put out a signal to stop the train. A red flag was used during the day and a red lantern at night.

Snow Removal

The rotary snow plough, a Canadian invention, came into use in 1888. When pushed by a couple of locomotives, the rotary plow could cut through deep drifts and blow the snow off the track.

The Roundhouse

The shop crew repaired locomotives in the roundhouse. Here a large turntable moved the heavy engines. Boys as young as 14 worked as wipers, cleaning and oiling the locomotives. A wiper kept the engine fire burning while a locomotive was being serviced in the roundhouse. If a boy was hard-working, he might move up to become a fireman and, eventually, an engineer.

DISASTER!

A t 4:35 A.M. on February 9, 1904, two CPR passenger trains crashed head-on at Sand Point, Ontario, killing 13 people and injuring at least 20 others. The eastbound train had not moved to a siding, as ordered, to allow the westbound train to pass. By the time the engineers caught sight of each other, no amount of braking could slow the trains in time. They collided with such force that the engines were locked together. Cars from behind "telescoped," or crashed through, the ones in front.

Six years later, on January 21, 1910, a passenger train derailed as it crossed a bridge over the Spanish River in Ontario. Forty-three passengers were killed and 38 others were seriously injured as four cars left the rails and hurtled down the embankment. One car caught fire on impact and two others plunged into the frozen river. Some passengers were burned, while others drowned struggling to free themselves from the wreck. A faulty piece of rail played a key role in this tragedy.

A dispatcher was responsible for scheduling and writing train orders for all trains in his division.

These accidents, while not typical of the early days of rail travel, were frightening. No matter how hard the railway worked to keep train travel safe, some disasters were inevitable. Brake failures, derailments, avalanches and human error were all things the early railway strove to overcome.

The railway company instituted many safety features to prevent accidents. They built double tracks, more sidings and snowsheds (to prevent avalanches from covering the tracks). They also operated a strict system of train orders. Train orders, telegraphed to the stations by the dispatchers, were the most important form of communication on the railway. They gave the engineer important safety information, such as when to move to a siding to allow another train to pass. A signalling system did not come into use until much later.

Sidings

When one train needed to pass another, the first train moved onto a siding — as instructed in the train orders. It waited there until the second train passed and the main track was clear again.

Trains could not be steered, so moveable pieces of track were used to move a train from one track to another.

The Spiral Tunnels

In the Rockies, a section of track called the Big Hill was so steep that trains had trouble going up or down it. Trains going up needed extra engines, called pushers, to help them. Trains going down had to travel slowly to avoid losing control. (The CPR built runaway tracks for emergencies, so that a runaway train could move off the main track to an uphill section of track.)

Trains were slowed in both directions, often causing bottlenecks or traffic jams. To solve the problem, the CPR built the Spiral Tunnels in 1909. Trains looped through gently sloping track in these tunnels. The extra distance they had to travel was better than facing the steep grade and long delays of the Big Hill.

FREIGHT TRAINS

The railway helped the country grow by providing quick and economical transportation of freight across the vast Canadian wilderness — something that had never before been possible.

Raw materials and manufactured goods from one part of Canada could now be sold in another part of the country or in the United States. Freight transportation played a key role in building the nation.

Many people, especially in isolated areas, also depended on the trains to deliver groceries, mail, tools and other supplies. The railway brought wood for building homes and barns and coal for fuel, as well as soap, coffee, cloth and other manufactured goods. It

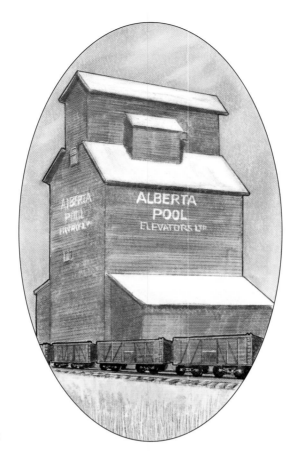

Wheat, stored in grain elevators near the station, was loaded and unloaded by hand. Wheat was Canada's most important export.

wasn't long before Eaton's catalogues found their way into train mailbags, so that settlers could order new clothing — to be delivered by train, of course!

Mixed trains included a combination of freight and passenger cars. They travelled between towns within one region rather than across the country. These small trains were often made up of a baggage-mail car, a cattle or other freight car, a boxcar hired by Eaton's or another company and a passanger coach.

The early freight trains transported freight such as coal, wheat, milk, lumber and cattle. With cheap and reliable transportation of these products, farming, ranching, mining and other industries grew quickly.

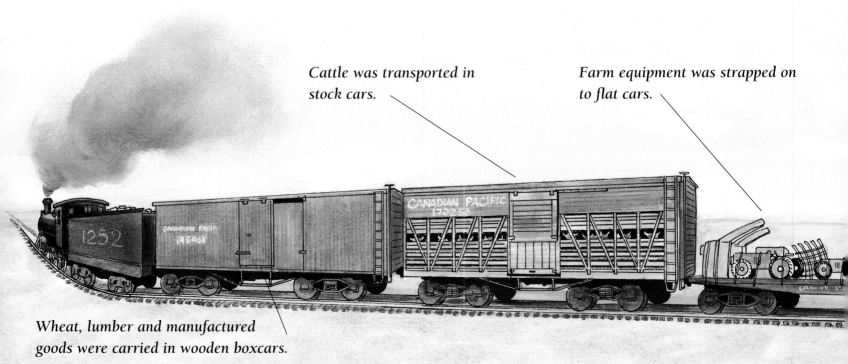

Cattle was transported in stock cars.

Farm equipment was strapped on to flat cars.

Wheat, lumber and manufactured goods were carried in wooden boxcars.

Inside the Caboose

The conductor and brakemen worked and slept in the caboose, which was like a home on wheels. Food, supplies, tools and safety equipment were carried in this car. Here the conductor wrote reports and kept track of which freight cars were to be picked up and dropped off.

The brakemen coupled and uncoupled the train cars. In the early days, they also set the handbrakes from the roof of each car when the engine brakes weren't strong enough to slow the train. This was dangerous work — if a man slipped and fell, he could be crushed beneath the moving train. By the 1900s, much safer air brakes were installed on all trains.

The conductor and brakemen took turns riding in the cupola. From here, they could inspect the cars, watch for danger and see the hand signals from the engine crew in front. In the days before radios, there were special hand signals for "stop," "back up," "go ahead" and many other tasks.

Tank cars held oil or other liquids.

The caboose was the last car on a freight train.

The cupola gave caboose crew a view of the train.

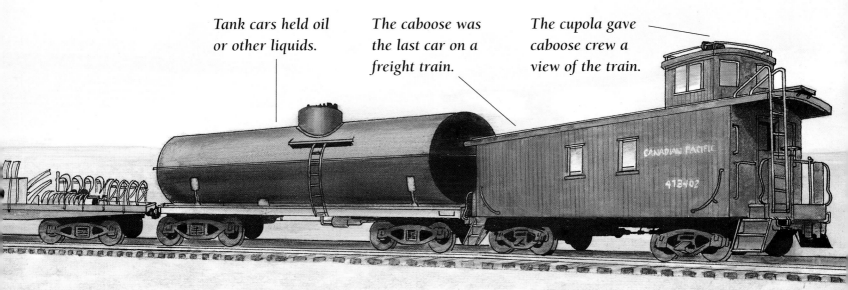

SPECIAL TRAINS

rains soon became the main transportation system across Canada, carrying people, goods and raw materials. Most trains made regular trips with passengers or freight, but some carried very special cargo.

From the early 1900s to the 1930s, fast-moving silk trains transported Asian silk from Vancouver to New York. The raw silk was so valuable — up to $10 million worth on a single train — that armed guards kept watch over it on its journey.

Like the silk trains, other special trains were made up as the need arose. Sometimes boxcars of food had to be sent to hungry people on the prairies. Other times, medical trains carried nurses and doctors to remote areas. School cars equipped with teachers and books took classes to students in the wilderness. And luxurious royal trains transported royalty on cross-country tours. Special trains were a unique part of Canada's past. Here are just a few of them.

Relief Trains

Many Canadians suffered during the Great Depression of the 1930s. Crop failures and a low price for wheat in the world market caused ten years of unemployment, food shortages and terrible hardship. Life was especially tough for people living on the prairies. Many families did not have enough to eat. To help feed them, relief trains were organized to transport boxcars of food from the east to the prairies.

School Cars

In the 1920s and 1930s and as late as 1967 in Ontario, school cars were sent to remote areas. A teacher travelling with the car taught children in one area for two or three days before moving on to another area.

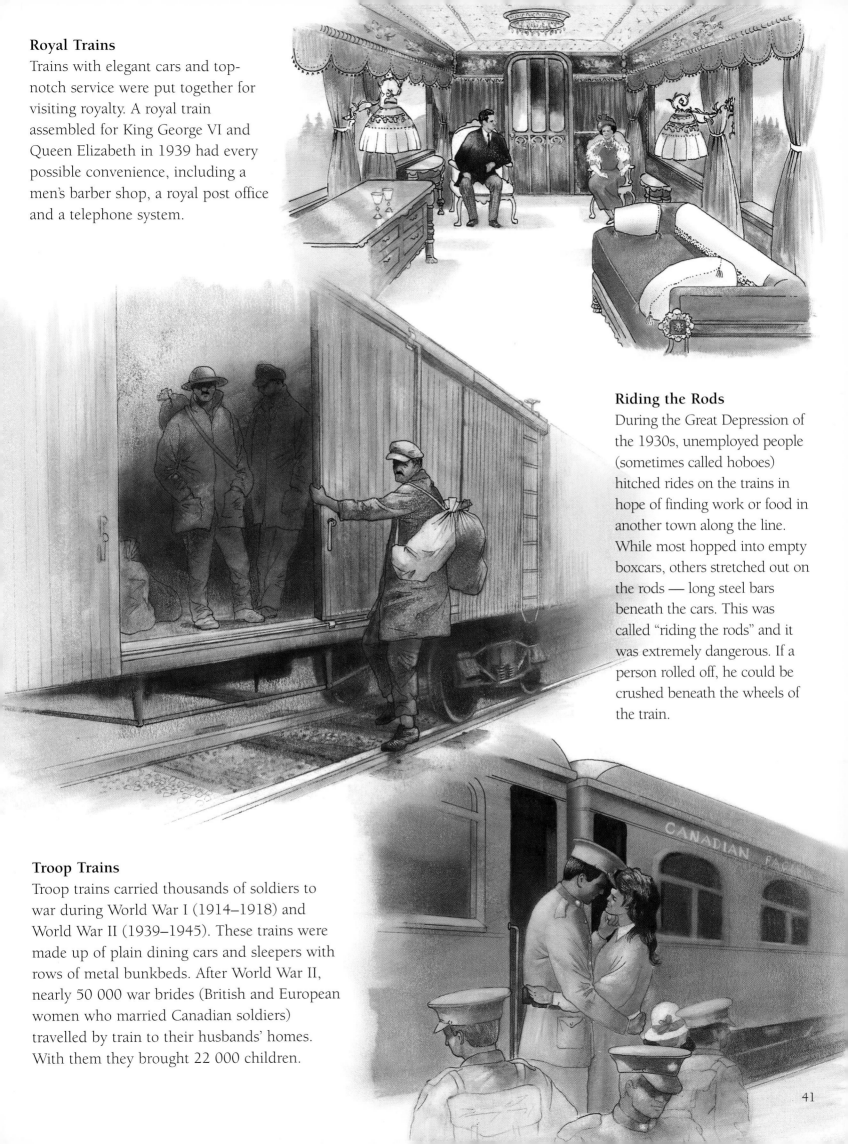

Royal Trains

Trains with elegant cars and top-notch service were put together for visiting royalty. A royal train assembled for King George VI and Queen Elizabeth in 1939 had every possible convenience, including a men's barber shop, a royal post office and a telephone system.

Riding the Rods

During the Great Depression of the 1930s, unemployed people (sometimes called hoboes) hitched rides on the trains in hope of finding work or food in another town along the line. While most hopped into empty boxcars, others stretched out on the rods — long steel bars beneath the cars. This was called "riding the rods" and it was extremely dangerous. If a person rolled off, he could be crushed beneath the wheels of the train.

Troop Trains

Troop trains carried thousands of soldiers to war during World War I (1914–1918) and World War II (1939–1945). These trains were made up of plain dining cars and sleepers with rows of metal bunkbeds. After World War II, nearly 50 000 war brides (British and European women who married Canadian soldiers) travelled by train to their husbands' homes. With them they brought 22 000 children.

TRAINS OVER TIME

The Canadian Pacific Railway was Canada's first transcontinental railway, but it was not the only one. In 1919, the Canadian National Railways (CNR) was created to take over several bankrupt railways. The new CNR formed a huge transcontinental railway system that spanned the country. In addition, branch lines — smaller railways that joined into larger ones — were built. With the growth of the railways, the population began spreading out across the country.

For many years, passenger trains were the fastest and most reliable way to travel. The railways did a bustling business and the CPR was one of Canada's major employers. However, when cars, trucks and airplanes became common, train travel dropped dramatically. As a result, the major railways (CPR and CNR) turned over passenger travel to Via Rail Canada in 1979. Today, Via Rail transports about 20 million passengers a year.

In contrast, freight trains became more important, transporting a large percentage of the goods shipped across the country. Today the CPR moves about 140 million tonnes (tons) of freight a year, including coal, sulphur, fertilizers, chemicals, grain, manufactured goods, forest and automotive products.

The Diesel Engine

After World War II, diesel engines began to replace steam locomotives. They didn't need to be refuelled as often, so they could travel distances in a shorter time. Running on oil, they were also cheaper and easier to operate. Diesels were operated by smaller crews. Workers such as firemen and wipers were no longer needed. Many lost their jobs. By the 1950s, the CPR and CNR had replaced all their steam engines with diesels.

Container Cargoes

Much of today's rail freight is shipped in containers or in truck trailers like the one above. Instead of having to load and unload cargo, the whole container or trailer can be transported from ships to trains and trucks. This saves work and keeps the cargo safe.

Network Management Centre

Train orders have been replaced with computers. Rail traffic controllers, in the Network Management Centre, send messages to the engineers by computer and radio. The computers track the position of trains all along the line.

Today's Trains

Although the trains have changed, riding in a modern passenger coach is still a good way to see Canada.

CANADA TODAY

Today, Canada is linked by railways, highways and airports. People move easily between cities and towns that stretch from coast to coast. Nearly 30 million people live here.

The transcontinental railways helped Canada become what it is today. Like a great band of steel, the CPR linked east and west and strengthened Canada in the early years of Confederation. Without the railway, much of Canada might have become part of the United States.

The railway, and the telegraph system built alongside it, allowed people to travel, communicate and transport goods and materials from one end of the country to the other. Passenger trains carried settlers to the prairies, and freight trains moved raw materials and manufactured items across Canada and into the United States. As a result, cities grew, and farms, ranches, mines and industries boomed.

Building the railway through the Canadian wilderness was an extraordinary feat — an almost impossible task in an almost impossible time. It was an accomplishment admired by people around the world. But the achievement was not without costs. Hundreds of railway workers died before the last spike was hammered in place, and the Métis and Aboriginal people lost their prairie lands and their independent way of life.

Despite these costs, the building of the railway had a dramatic effect on the growth of the country. Many people believe that the railway shaped the nation.

Cities and towns border the railway
routes from east to west across the country.

The Last Spike Memorial

Today, a marker at Craigellachie, British Columbia (near Revelstoke), reminds people of the enormous challenge of building the transcontinental railway over a hundred years ago. The plaque reads, "Here was driven the last spike completing Canadian Pacific Railway from ocean to ocean November 7 1885."

William Cornelius Van Horne

To honour his role in building the railway, Van Horne was knighted in 1894 and became Sir William Cornelius Van Horne. He died on September 11, 1915. On the day of his funeral, all CPR trains stopped for five minutes.

RAILWAY FACTS

- Canada's earliest railway may have been built on Cape Breton Island in the 1720s. Remains in the area suggest that horse-drawn carts, guided by simple wooden rails, transported building materials for the fortress of Louisbourg.

- A horse-drawn railway was also used in the 1820s to move stone during the building of the Quebec Citadel, another fortress.

- In 1864, George M. Pullman invented the sleeping car for trains. Today sleeping cars are often called Pullman cars.

- Early CPR logos displayed a beaver. The beaver was chosen to represent the hard-working nature of the railway company.

- When diesel-powered trains were new, people didn't recognize the sound of their horns at crossings. This was unsafe, so a Canadian inventor named Robert Swanson developed an airhorn that copied the sound of a steam engine's whistle.

- There are about 24 000 railway crossings in Canada.

- The CPR route has 80 tunnels and 3000 bridges.

- The longest tunnel in the western hemisphere is Mount MacDonald in British Columbia. It is 14.6 km (9 mi.) long.

- The longest, highest railway bridge in Canada is the Lethbridge Viaduct in Alberta. It is 1624 m (5328 ft.) long and 96 m (315 ft.) high.

- The busiest section of the CPR is from Calgary to Vancouver, where the railway hauls about 34 million tonnes (tons) of coal a year.

- Today, the CNR is the largest railway in Canada. The CPR is the second largest.

- The CPR employs 24 000 workers.

- The CPR owns 1600 locomotives and 48 000 freight cars. It spends nearly a billion dollars a year in maintenance, repairs and improvements.

- A freight train with 150 cars, travelling at 50 km/h (30 m.p.h.) needs a distance of about 1600 m (1750 yd.) to stop.

- The same train travelling at 80 km/h (50 m.p.h.) would take up to two minutes to come to a complete stop.

- A train whistle of two long blasts, one short and one long blast means: "Stop! A train is approaching."

- Trains always have the right of way over vehicles at crossings.

- Today, people in large cities such as Montreal, Toronto and Vancouver can ride on electric- or diesel-powered high speed trains. These trains transport people from the suburbs to downtown centres.

WORDS FROM THE PAST

bird cage: caboose. Also known as bone breaker, cigar box, crummy and doghouse.

brakie: brakeman

deadhead: a locomotive that ran alone, without cars or a caboose

deadheader: an engineer, conductor or trainman who rode, but didn't work on, another crew's train

extra: a train put on a run in addition to regularly scheduled trains

flimsies: train orders

gandy dancer: a railway worker who built or maintained the track

hog: the engine

hogger: the engineer

milk run: a train that made frequent stops. The term came from trains that stopped to pick up cans of milk from farms all along the line.

navvy: a railway construction worker. The name was borrowed from workers who built early navigation canals.

silker: a train that transported silk

tie down the brakes: set the handbrakes

whistle stop: a small, unimportant town along the railway line

INDEX